12.96

MW00952929

The Inuit

by Allison Lassieur

Consultant:
John F. Pingayak
Cultural Heritage Director
Kashunamiut School District
Chevak, Alaska

Bridgestone Books
an imprint of Capstone Press
Mankato, Minnesota

Bridgestone Books are published by Capstone Press
151 Good Counsel Drive, P.O. Box 669, Mankato, Minnesota 56002
http://www.capstone-press.com

Library of Congress Cataloging-in-Publication Data
Lassieur, Allison.
      The Inuit/by Allison Lassieur.
      p. cm.—(Native peoples)
      Includes bibliographical references and index.
      Summary: An overview of the Inuit and a description of their homes, food, clothing,
art, family life, storytelling, religion, and government.
      ISBN 0-7368-0498-6
      1. Inuit—History—Juvenile literature. 2. Inuit—Social life and customs—Juvenile
literature. [1. Inuit. 2. Eskimos.] I. Series.
E99.E7 L289 2000
971.9'0049712—dc21   99-052065

Editorial Credits

Rebecca Glaser, editor; Timothy Halldin, cover designer and illustrator; Sara A. Sinnard,
   illustrator; Kimberly Danger, photo researcher

Photo Credits

Lawrence Migdale, 14
Lyn Hancock, 8, 12
Robin Karpan, cover, 10
Visuals Unlimited/McCutcheon, 16, 18, 20
Yvette Cardozo, 6

1 2 3 4 5 6 05 04 03 02 01 00

Table of Contents

Russia

Siberia

Arctic Circle

Alaska

Nunavut

Northwest Territories

Canada

Greenland

United States

Traditional Location

About 125,000 Inuit live in the world. Most Inuit live in the Arctic areas of the United States, Canada, Russia, and Greenland. A few Inuit live in large cities in the United States, Canada, and Russia.

Fast Facts

The Inuit are indigenous people of northern Alaska, Canada, Greenland, and Siberia. Indigenous means that they have always lived there. Today, Inuit live like many other North Americans. The Inuit are proud of their past traditions. These facts tell about the Inuit in the past and today.

Homes: In the past, the Inuit built houses from driftwood, stones, whale bones, sod, or snow. Today, most Inuit live in modern wooden homes. The Inuit word for any kind of house is iglu or ena.

Food: In the past, the Inuit lived off the land. They hunted and fished. They ate caribou, walrus, seal, and whale meat. Today, they still depend on these animals for meat. But other foods also are available. The Inuit can buy fruit, vegetables, and packaged foods such as potato chips in local stores.

Clothing: Years ago, the Inuit wore parkas, leggings, and boots made from animal skins and fur. They wore layers of clothing to keep warm. Today, the Inuit wear clothes like those of other North Americans. But they still need to wear heavy outer clothing for the cold arctic weather.

Language: The Inuit in Alaska and in the Siberian region of Russia speak Yup'ik, Cup'ik, Siberian Yup'ik, or Inupiaq. The Inuit in Canada speak Inuktitut. The Inuit in Greenland speak Greenlandic.

Inuit History

The Inuit have always lived in the Arctic. They lived off the land. They hunted seals, whales, and caribou. They also fished. The Inuit ate the meat from these animals. They made clothes from the skins and furs. They made tools from the animals' bones.

European explorers first came to Inuit lands in the 1500s. The explorers were looking for a shortcut from the Atlantic Ocean to the Pacific Ocean.

Europeans continued to come to Inuit lands. In the 1800s, fur traders and whalers hunted animals until the animals were almost gone. In the early 1900s, European missionaries brought the religion of Christianity to the Inuit.

Europeans claimed Inuit lands as their own. The lands had valuable resources such as oil and gold. The Inuit fought to keep their lands. In the late 1900s, both Canada and the United States gave land back to the Inuit. Today, Inuit groups have their own governments and control their own land.

The Inuit have always fished for food.

The Inuit

In the past, the Inuit were known as Eskimos. Eskimo is an Ojibwa Indian word. It means "to net snowshoes." Inuit means "the people" in Inuktitut. Most Inuit prefer this name. In Alaska, each Inuit group chooses its own name. Inupiat, Cup'ik, and Yup'ik are names of some groups.

Today, most Inuit live like others in North America. They live in small towns. They have jobs. They buy food at grocery stores. Inuit children go to school. But many Inuit still fish and hunt for food. The whole town celebrates after a successful hunt.

The Inuit work hard to keep their traditions. Every year, Inuit from all over the Arctic come together for the Northern Games. They compete in contests like fish cutting, seal skinning, and the high kick. The Inuit also are preserving their languages. Some television programs in Canada are broadcast in Inuktitut. Inuit children learn their traditional language in school.

The Inuit compete in the Northern Games, which are held each summer.

The Amautiq

Inuit women often carry their babies on their backs in an amautiq. This device doubles as a parka and keeps the baby warm next to the mother's body. In the past, women made amautiqs from animal skins and furs. Today, women use amautiqs made from cotton.

Homes, Food, and Clothing

Years ago, the Inuit built many types of houses. Inuit who lived near coasts built homes from sod and whale bones or rocks. Some Inuit stretched caribou skins over a wooden frame to make their homes. Some put up summer tents made of seal skins. Inuit used snow houses mainly while hunting. Today, most Inuit live in modern wooden houses.

In the past, the Inuit ate seal, walrus, caribou, and whale meat. This diet gave the Inuit energy to survive the cold. The meat from these animals is full of vitamins. Today, many Inuit still hunt and eat a lot of meat. They also buy food at grocery stores.

Years ago, Inuit women made clothes from animal skins and furs. Men and women wore coats called parkas. They also wore fur leggings, boots, and mittens. In very cold weather, the Inuit wore two layers of clothes. The air between the layers held in body heat. Today, many Inuit wear modern clothes. But they still wear fur clothes to keep warm.

Inuit Art

Hundreds of years ago, the Inuit decorated almost everything they owned. They decorated clothing with patterns of different colored fur. They carved pictures into handles of hunting tools. The Inuit believed that the beauty of their hunting tools made animal spirits happy.

Today, the Inuit are famous for their art. Many Inuit carve figures out of soapstone, bone, or ivory. Some Inuit artists paint pictures. Other Inuit decorate fur clothing with colorful trim. Inuit artwork often shows arctic animals. Other artwork uses pictures to tell Inuit stories. This art shows the respect that the Inuit have for their traditions.

Some Inuit villages have art cooperatives. These groups buy Inuit art and sell it to people all over the world. Some Inuit make a living by selling their artwork.

Inuit sculptors often carve arctic animals from soapstone.

Inuit Families

In the past, the Inuit lived in small groups. A few families made up each group. The Inuit shared everything with their family and friends. They divided food from a hunt so that every family received some meat.

To survive in the Arctic, every family member had a job to do. Men hunted walruses, seals, whales, and caribou. They also made tools and other useful objects. Boys helped at home until they were old enough to hunt. Women and girls dried the animal skins and meat after a hunt. They cooked food and sewed clothing. Children worked with their parents to learn the Inuit ways of life.

Inuit families no longer can live off the land alone. They need to buy items the land does not provide. Today, many Inuit have jobs in schools, village stores, or in the government.

Many Inuit families shop for food and household goods in village stores.

Inuit Storytelling

Very few Inuit stories have been written down. The Inuit passed on their stories by telling them out loud. The Inuit told stories to pass time during the long, dark winters. Many stories taught values and lessons about life. Today, the Inuit elders continue to tell their stories. Stories often are told with songs and dances.

In the past, many Inuit girls played a special storytelling game. They used an object called a storyknife. A storyknife is a piece of carved bone or ivory. Most Inuit fathers carved beautiful storyknives for their daughters.

Inuit girls sat in a circle on the ground to play the game. A girl smoothed the ground with her storyknife. She then began her story. She drew pictures in the ground with the storyknife as she told her story. The girls took turns making up stories. They told stories about animals, their families, or each other.

Inuit elders tell stories with dances.

Inuit Religion

Today, many Inuit believe in Christianity. This religion follows the teachings of Jesus Christ.

The Inuit also have other beliefs. They believe that all living things have a spirit. When a hunter kills an animal, the hunter asks its spirit to return to the world. The spirit will become angry if a hunter does not speak to an animal's spirit. Animals then no longer come to Inuit lands.

In the past, the Inuit believed that some people could travel to the spirit world. These people were called angalkuqs, or shamans. Angalkuqs brought back the spirits of large schools of fish or animals. This ensured there would be plenty of food the following spring and summer.

For many years, the Inuit did not practice their own religion. The beliefs faded away. Now more Inuit are learning about the old beliefs. Some Inuit families practice these beliefs in their homes. The Inuit are slowly bringing back the ways of the past.

The Inuit hunt whales for blubber and meat. After a hunter kills an animal, he asks its spirit to return to the world.

Inuit Government

Hundreds of years ago, the Inuit did not have a government. Instead, they chose strong hunters to be their leaders.

Over the years, Inuit leaders have worked to reclaim Inuit lands. In 1971, the United States returned 44 million acres (18 million hectares) of Alaskan land to the Inuit and other Native Americans. In 1993, Canada created a territory called Nunavut. The Inuit who live there control their government. The U.S. and Canadian governments also gave money to the Inuit.

Today, every Inuit village has a tribal council. The council makes laws for the village. Most communities have city offices. City offices manage the money received from national governments.

Village corporations operate stores and buy oil and gas for a village. Village corporations are part of larger regional corporations. The regional corporations work to protect the region's land.

Tribal councils meet to make decisions for villages.

Hands On: Make Snow Goggles

Snow covers arctic lands for much of the year. Sunshine on white snow can hurt a person's eyes. The Inuit once wore snow goggles to help them see better in bright light. They made snow goggles from bone or wood.

What You Need

Heavy paper or posterboard
Scissors
Crayons, pencils, or paint

Paper punch
String

What You Do

1. Cut a glasses shape out of the heavy paper or posterboard. It should be about the same width as your face. The glasses should cover only your eyes.
2. Cut two horizontal slits in the glasses. You should be able to see out of the slits.
3. Decorate the mask with crayons, pencils, or paint.
4. Punch a hole on each side of the mask.
5. Tie a piece of string in each hole. Put on your goggles and tie them behind your head.

The slits are small enough to keep bright light away from your eyes. The slits are large enough to see through. Inuit hunters used snow goggles like these when they hunted during the day. Today, most Inuit hunters wear sunglasses.

Words to Know

Angalkuq (a-NGUTHL-kook)—a religious person who has the power to talk to the spirit world

caribou (KAYR-uh-boo)—a large member of the deer family; caribou have antlers and live mostly in the Arctic.

Christianity (krist-chee-AN-uh-tee)—a religion based on the life and teachings of Jesus Christ

corporation (kor-puh-RAY-shuhn)—a group of people who are in charge of a company or town

council (KOUN-suhl)—a group of leaders

missionary (MISH-uh-nair-ee)—a person who teaches a certain religion to others

religion (ri-LIJ-uhn)—a set of spiritual beliefs that people follow

soapstone (SOHP-stone)—a soft stone with a soapy feel often used for carving

sod (SAHD)—the top layer of soil and the grass attached to it

traditional (truh-DISH-uhn-uhl)—having to do with the past

Read More

Alexander, Bryan and Cherry. *What Do We Know About the Inuit?* New York: Peter Bedrick Books, 1995.

Harper, Judith E. *Inuit.* Mankato, Minn.: Smart Apple Media, 1999.

Thomson, Ruth. *The Inuit.* Footsteps in Time. New York: Children's Press, 1996.

Useful Addresses

Inuit Circumpolar Conference
170 Laurier Avenue West
Suite 504
Ottawa, ON K1P 5V5
Canada

Yupiit Piciryarait Cultural Center and Museum
420 State Highway
P.O. Box 219
Bethel, AK 99559

Internet Sites

Alaska Native Heritage Center
http://www.alaskanative.net
Alaska Native Language Center
http://www.uaf.edu/anlc/index.html
Alaska Native Studies Curriculum and Teacher Development
http://www.alaskool.org
Canadian Museum of Civilization
http://www.civilization.ca/membrs/fph/stones/welcome.htm
The Nunavut Handbook
http://www.arctictravel.com

Index